YES...YOU
HOW TO RIDE A MOT
By Chris Torti

CHAPTERS

CHAPTER ONE
INTRODUCTION

I began riding motorcycles at the age of 55. I didn't want to ride motorcycles at age 55, or any other age for that matter. No, I did not have a burning desire left over from my youth to mount an iron stallion and feel the wind in my hair and the bugs in my teeth. I wasn't a Hell's Angels wannabe. No, it was much simpler than that. I began riding because my wife at the time wanted to ride, or more accurately, be a passenger while I rode. She had to do an awful lot of convincing to get me to sign on to this crazy idea, because I was sure I would get one or both of us killed. I did not consider myself all that great a skilled driver of a car, and was sure that on a motorcycle I would meet with disaster. I envisioned myself being too stressed and nervous to enjoy the experience.

I needn't have worried. I took the motorcycle safety course offered by my dealer, in this case Harley-Davidson, and fell in love with riding. If you are new to riding and you haven't taken this, or a similar, course, I strongly urge you to do so and will have more on that subject in the next chapter.

I told you my story for a reason. We all get into motorcycling for different reasons. In my case I was coerced. If you are reading this book because you are thinking of riding or have already started, you have your own motivation for wanting to do so. My point is it really doesn't matter. Once you start doing it you will love it or you won't, but what you will learn is that it isn't hard. As they told us in the beginning of the safety course, if you can ride a bicycle, you can ride a motorcycle. The principles of balance and physics are the same. Once you master the clutch, throttle, and brakes you are ready to ride...and it does not take long to get enough of a handle on those three things as you are probably thinking it will.

I do not want to trivialize the skill necessary to become a really good rider. And I certainly don't want to lead you to believe that you do not need to utilize extraordinary caution when out on the highways on a two-wheeler (or three-wheeler), because what are minor mishaps in an automobile can become life threatening situations on a motorcycle.

That first motorcycle course was over eight years ago, and I have since logged over 90,000 miles on a motorcycle. My first bike was a 2004 Harley-Davidson Road King, which my son now owns. I put 11,500 miles on that bike in the first six months before letting him have it for what was owed on it while I bought a brand new 2006 H-D Electra Glide Ultra Classic, which I still own and has 79,000 miles on it. We also had a 2005 Honda VTX1300 (which my son-in-law now has) and a 2004 Honda Shadow that I put a few miles on, but not many.

So, you see, I tried something I was literally scared to death of doing, ended up loving it, and then both my son and son-in-law started riding too and this has led to a lot of family fun over the past several years.

Many older riders had ridden early in their lives, but marriage and kids came along and they turned their bikes in for minivans, or some such family conveyance. Years later, the kids grown and gone and life getting a little dull, many end up coming back to riding. These riders can benefit from this book as well as new riders...and also from taking the safety class. They will pick it up again fairly quickly, quicker than the new rider in most cases, but it is good to re-familiarize themselves with the operation of a motorcycle and how you can reduce your risk of accidents.

I want to spend the rest of this book sharing with you some of the things I've learned...some of them the hard way...some of them the scary way...and some of them just from plain, old experience. I hope you enjoy reading what follows and we'll get back together in the end to wrap it up.

CHAPTER TWO
TRAINING

I spoke of the Riders' Safety Course that is offered by most motorcycle dealerships. You do not have to buy a bike to take the course there. Just go in, sign up, pay your money, and show up. I did not buy any of my bikes at that dealership, but used it for servicing my Ultra.

The courses vary in length depending upon the entity giving the course. The one I took at Central Texas Harley-Davidson (at that time in Austin, Texas but now in Round Rock, Texas) was four days long and was called "The Rider's Edge". The first two nights were classroom work, followed by a fifty question written exam (which I aced by getting all fifty right, I might add). The weekend was for riding in the parking lot, which was followed by a final riding exam (which I did not ace, but did well enough to pass).

In Texas, and in many other states I'm sure; the certificate of completion you receive exempts you from having to take the riding part of the drivers' license test for a motorcycle endorsement on your driver's license. So right there the investment was worth it to me.

Classroom

The very first thing we were taught, and it was pounded home, was that in deciding that you want to ride motorcycles you are accepting a higher level of risk. As previously mentioned, a minor mishap in a car or truck ("cages" in biker parlance), like a flat tire for example, can be a major mishap on a motorcycle. A fender bender in a cage that results in no injuries at all can seriously harm a biker and/or a passenger.

Another short terminology side trip: the "driver" of the motorcycle is called the rider and the "passenger" is called the passenger. Being the passenger is sometimes referred to as "riding bitch", but that's for another book. Two people on a motorcycle are referred to as "riding two-up".

There is a workbook that accompanies the classroom sessions of the course. It is loaded with good information, and the final exam comes directly from it. The final is easy as long as you pay attention and study the workbook.

In the classroom we studied safety equipment and learned what kinds are better than other kinds. We will get into this in greater detail later on.

We also learned how to shift a motorcycle, something that had always been confusing to me until then. A motorcycle shifter is a foot shifter on the left hand side of the bike. The clutch is a hand lever, also on the left side of the bike. The equipment that makes the bike go is on the left side of the bike. The equipment that makes the bike stop is on the right hand side. The front brake lever is on the right handlebar and the rear brake foot pedal is on the right side.

Anyway, back to the shifter. Most motorcycles have five or six gears. You step on the shifter to push it down to the bottom gear, which is first gear. You do this while depressing the clutch handle. Then, one click up is second gear. You click the shifter up and then let it go. When you are ready to shift again, you depress the clutch and shift up and release the clutch. You are now in third gear. You repeat this process until you are in your bike's top gear. Neutral is located half a click up from first gear (or half a click down from second gear). Learning clutch and throttle control to insure smooth shifting and acceleration takes practice, and like a car, differs from bike to bike. Once you are riding your own bike you will quickly become familiar with the sensitivity of your clutch and your throttle. You will also use your shifter for slowing the bike down in preparation for stopping. Downshifting allows the rider to always keep control of the bike during the stopping process and also extends the life of the brake pads by letting the engine do the work. You do not want to shift the bike into neutral and coast to a stop because you never know when you may need a burst of acceleration to avoid another vehicle and you don't want to take time to shift the bike into gear.

In class we also discussed physics as it relates to keeping a motorcycle upright and on the road. One maxim that becomes very apparent once you start riding is that speed increases stability. A motorcycle moving down the highway ay 70 mph is extremely stable. But one slowing to a stop, or sitting at a stop is very unstable. Imagine a coin that you place on its edge on a table and then flick with your finger. It stays upright as long as it is spinning at high speed. But as the spinning slows the coin starts to tilt, and then wobble, and then finally fall over. We will discuss this concept more and apply it to actual riding situations later.

Other important things we learned were how to go through turns; proper lane positioning for different situations; how to stop your bike in a hurry; but most importantly we learned about defensive riding, something I will spend a lot of time on later in the book as well.

Parking Lot

The first thing they told us once outside in the parking lot was that when we completed this course we would be certified to ride in a parking lot. This was true. There was no traffic, no crazy drivers (other than ourselves), no stop signs or traffic signals…just twenty neophyte riders and a bunch of cones and lines painted on the asphalt.

We were all given Buell motorcycles, which at the time was a division of Harley-Davidson. The Buell's were H-D's attempt to compete for the crotch rocket market. The H-D Racing Team used them too. They were small and light and perfect for learning on. I have observed courses at other dealerships and all different kinds of bikes were being used, but the one thing they all had in common was, for the most part, they were all small and light and easy to handle from a weight and balance perspective.

We began with something the instructors called "power walking". This was actually a lot of fun, and was my very first hint that I might actually like this. With your feet on the ground you straddled the bike with it in first gear and the clutch depressed. The idea was to get used to clutch control. The objective was to let out enough clutch so the bike moved forward but you were still able to "walk" the bike. The more we did this the better we got at it. It was a great way of building some confidence that you will be able to control the momentum of the motorcycle and to understand how sensitive the clutch is and how much reaction the bike has to it.

From there we graduated to actually riding the bikes in large ovals with the admonishment that we do not shift above second gear. This got us use to moving under the power of the engine and making one gear shift. It also taught us about leaning through turns. Motorcycles only steer with the handlebars when they are sitting still or moving very slowly. All other times the bike's direction is changed by leaning the bike to the side you want it to go to. You actually do this by pressing down slightly on the handlebar grip to get the bike to lean over on that side. The faster you are going the farther over you can safely lean and the tighter your turn will be.

Now here is where I must make a confession. I am a slow learner. This should give you hope because I figure it took me twice as long as the average rider to become proficient at riding motorcycles. I have to make a mistake a couple of times before the solution, or proper method, becomes apparent to me. As well as I did in the classroom (something I've had lots of experience in); I did the opposite out in the parking lot.

In the classroom discussion on physics we were told to never apply the brakes while leaning the bike. This brings the bike to an abrupt halt, and if it is still leaning over its going over…and you are going off. And I did this twice. The first time the instructor complimented me on a very nice shoulder-roll to escape injury. The second time, about 30 minutes later, he cursed me for being too stupid to ride and expressed real concern that I was going to get myself killed once I got out on the highway.

I was depressed and wanted to quit right then and there. Plus, on the second fall the bike came down on the back of my foot and my ankle was bruised and hurting. No great shoulder-roll on that one. I couldn't understand why this was happening. I truly did not remember that classroom discussion about brakes and leaning, and no one corrected me on the course and I kept doing it. Fortunately the Buell's are light bikes and I was able to hold it up by getting my foot down in a hurry and straddling it, but every stop was jerky and not smooth like it should have been. In the final I got points deducted for my stops and I still didn't realize this was because I wasn't bringing my bike perfectly upright before braking. Later in the book I will give you other examples of my slow learning abilities.

We also practiced riding over objects in the roadway (short pieces of 2x4 boards); changing lanes and using our blinkers; riding through obstacle courses super slowly (making it difficult to keep the bike up and you couldn't put your feet down or swing outside the lines). But the amazing thing was the more we did this the better we got at it. By the time the second morning was concluded we all felt pretty proficient with riding in a parking lot and being able to handle all of the things we were going to have to demonstrate on the final. I don't think I had ever been more nervous about any kind of test before.

The test began after lunch and I do not recall how many tasks we had to complete, but points were deducted for each thing you did wrong. I believe if you got 20 points deducted you failed the final. One guy in the class had ridden years before and had quit for one reason or another but was going to start up again and decided to take the test to see how his skills were. He was far and away the best in the class and he aced the final and the instructor used him to demonstrate the proper way to go through the obstacle course. A couple other students had less than five points deducted. The rest of us were between 5 and 18 or so. I had 11. No one failed. We had a little graduation ceremony and received our certificates of completion exempting us from the riding portion of the license test. I was ecstatic with an overwhelming sense of accomplishment that I had succeeded in doing something I was very nervous about trying and finding out I really liked it. I was 55 years old, the oldest student in the class, and ready to get my first motorcycle!

CHAPTER THREE
PICKING THE RIGHT BIKE

You probably have an idea of the kind of bike you want to buy already if you have been thinking about riding for any length of time. Many people worry that they are not strong enough or big enough to handle larger motorcycles, and often make the mistake of buying a bike that quickly becomes too small, or not enough bike, for them.

This fear is often unfounded. Motorcycles are incredibly balanced, and are easier to hold upright than you might think. Oh sure, you'll let it tip over a time or two while you are learning, but that almost always happens when you are at a stop (remember speed=stability). When that happens you'll be a little embarrassed, but you won't hurt the bike as almost all bigger bikes have engine guards (or "crash bars" as they are sometimes referred to), and the smaller, lighter bikes are easier to keep from tipping over. The engine guards will hold the bike at about a 45-degree angle and you lift it back up and go on your way. If you don't have the strength to get it back upright, get someone else to help you. I've never encountered the motorcycle that couldn't be lifted upright by two people. After some experience is gained and you become more familiar with your bike's balance a tip over becomes a rarity…but I have seen it happen to some of the most experienced bikers, so it is nothing to be embarrassed about.

The most important thing is fit. You are going to spend a lot of time on your motorcycle, and in needs to fit your body size comfortably. It's just like a pair of shoes. No matter how good they look, if they are not the right size they are going to hurt, leave blisters, and you are going to tire of them quickly and start leaving them in your closet. Your investment in a motorcycle is a significant one, for most people, anyway. You need to make sure you choose a bike that is comfortable, the right size, the right amount of power and you love the way it looks.

One of the most important things to consider in fitting yourself to a motorcycle is how high off the ground the seat is. The lower the bike, the lower its center of gravity and the more stable it is. But the real reason you need to know this is because you need to be able to straddle the bike while standing up in order to hold it upright for a passenger to mount. The test for this is to sit on the bike and place your feet flat on the ground. If your legs are slightly bent at the knees than this is an acceptable height for you. If they are out straight, you need a lower bike. This is often an issue for shorter riders, and most often women.

Among Harley-Davidson models, women are often encouraged toward the Sportster, because it is smaller and both of its engine choices (883 and 1200) are smaller than Harley's standard engine in its other models. However, the Sportster is higher off the ground than most of the Dyna models, and the Dynas often offer a better fit for shorter riders than the Sportster. Also, the smaller engine can be misleading. The lightweight of the Sportster more than compensates for the smaller engine and they are extremely quick. So, if you are thinking smaller engine for less speed, think again.

Another important fit-factor to consider is the seat. Do not go on looks alone. If the seat isn't comfortable the ride will be a chore and eventually something you dread. You'll park your bike in the garage and eventually sell it, and all that could have been avoided with the selection of a comfortable seat. Remember, you do not have to take the stock seat that comes on the bike. You can have the dealer replace it with a seat you like better. Of course, trying out seats is kind of like tying out mattresses. It can feel good during a five-minute tryout, and not so good after two hours of being on it. So, if you try out different bikes before buying, try to find bikes with different seats so you will have an idea of which seats you like better. If you buy a bike and later decide you don't like the seat, you can always buy a different seat that fits your model.

These principles apply to all makes, models, and kinds of motorcycles. I am most familiar with Harley-Davidson's so I feel confident making comparisons between their four traditional classes of motorcycles (Sportster, Dyna, Softail, and Touring). I say traditional because they have added a special category for V-Rods and one for larger engine touring bikes called CVO. But for the purposes of our discussion here, the four classes I mention above will suffice…and almost all brands of motorcycles will have models in similar classes, so if you want a Honda or a Victory or a Boulevard, some simple research will give you the facts you need to properly compare the various models and classes.

I chose Harley-Davidson for two reasons. When someone learns you have a motorcycle the first question they ask is inevitably, "Is it a Harley?" As if no other bike counts, which of course, is not the case. But the fact remains; Harley-Davidson is the most well known motorcycle on the market. The second reason was I could afford it. You can get a very good motorcycle of similar size and specs for about half the price you'll pay for a Harley. But no other model retains its value like a Harley-Davidson. When it comes time to sell or trade in your bike, you can get close to what you paid for it. I bought my 2006 Ultra Classic in December of 2005 and I paid $20,500.00 for it in stock condition (no extras added on). Now after I added the extras and bought a service plan I ended up paying $29,000.00, but that was all my choice. I could have ridden it out of the showroom right out of the box for $20,500.00. Today, 8 years (the 2014 models are out) and 79,000 miles later, the Kelly Blue Book value of my motorcycle is $12,870.00. I could take that money and buy a brand new Suzuki or Yamaha or Victory and not spend a dime of my own money. Or, I could put it towards a newer model Harley.

Another reason I chose Harley-Davidson is that it is an American company with a great story. A family-owned business started in Milwaukee, Wisconsin in the early years (1903) of brand motorcycle production. With the exception of thirteen years when the company was owned by AMF (yes, the bowling alley people), a period when the quality suffered and the reputation nearly ruined, this company has flourished and has been an American success story. I've ridden other motorcycles and I just like the feel and ride of the Harleys better. But that's just my opinion, and certainly not shared by all, and definitely not by the folks who own bikes other than Harley-Davidsons.

You probably have noticed that many state and local police and sheriff's departments have switched from Harley-Davidsons to other models, most notably BMW's. Many of the motor officers I have talked to like the BMW's better. Easier to handle, lighter, faster, and they were the first motorcycle to come out with ABS brakes. The bigger Harleys have them now as standard equipment, but BMW had them first. Controlled braking is extremely important, especially for a motor officer who finds himself in a high-speed chase...or just riding in heavy traffic or in wet or icy road conditions. An Automatic Braking System ensures that your brakes won't lock your wheels up causing you to go into a skid. If you don't have ABS brakes, also known as anti-locking brakes, then you need to be especially mindful of how you engage your front and rear brakes. If you are just normally coming to a slow controlled stop at a traffic light or stop sign, I find it best to first downshift to use my engine to slow the speed of my bike. By the time I get down to second gear the bike is moving pretty slow and I bring it to a stop with the rear (foot) brakes, using my hand brake to make the final stop and hold the bike in position, if needed. But if you need to make a quick stop for any reason, you hit both brakes simultaneously while downshifting the transmission. A motorcycle requires less distance than a car to stop at the same speed. In other words, a bike can stop quicker than a car. But if you don't control your stop you can have far more disastrous results than a car will have. Using the method I described above vastly decreases the chances of your bike going into a sideways skid, and keeps the bike in a straight line during the stop.

Another item to look at are the handlebars. What feels comfortable to you? Are your arms stretched out too much? Can you reach the far grip when the wheel is turned to its maximum? Do you like the level your hands are at? Bars come in all sizes and shapes. Try several out and go with the most comfortable. Sometimes bars that look uncomfortable are actually quite the opposite.

Finding the bike that is right for you is extremely important. You want to be in love with your motorcycle, and you won't be if you are not totally comfortable on it. And not just fit, but size of the engine, weight of the bike, sound of the exhaust, carburetor of fuel injected, all of these things will come into play in deciding whether you love your bike or not. The good news is all of these things are fixable if you want something different. But the hardest thing to fix is bike height so get that one right from the beginning.

CHAPTER FOUR
SAFETY EQUIPMENT

Let's face it; if you get in a wreck on a motorcycle, even a minor one, you can sustain some serious bodily injury. Even minor bodily injury, such as "road rash" (skin abrasion from scraping the asphalt) can be painful and an extreme nuisance. The safety equipment we are going to discuss in this chapter may or may not save your life, but it can certainly go a long way towards minimizing injury.

Every time I see a rider riding along in shorts and flip-flops I want to cringe. When I see him with a girl on the back dressed the same way, I know he's not considerate of her safety. If he wants to take the risk of riding, and crashing, dressed like that it's his choice. The passenger may not know any better. He at least has the responsibility of informing her that a second layer of skin made of denim or leather can at least save her from weeks of discomfort if they were to go down. If she still decides to ride with no protection, well, that is her choice. Remember we said that riding is to accept a higher level of risk. That is just as true for the passenger as it is the rider. I feel that the rider is responsible for the passenger's safety, and that includes insuring that he/she is dressed in a protective manner, or understands the consequences.

Helmets

The first item we'll talk about is a helmet. This is the most obvious piece of protective equipment, and one of the most controversial. Whenever someone has a motorcycle wreck the first question always seems to be, "Was he wearing a helmet?" Whenever a report of a fatal motorcycle accident is reported in the newspaper, and the rider was not wearing a helmet, you always see that fact reported. Like if he was wearing a helmet he'd be alive today. But if he was wearing one you never see, "Mr. Smith was wearing a helmet, but died anyway." Some states have helmet laws, requiring riders and passengers to wear helmets. Most states have helmet laws that only require riders and passengers under the age of 18 to wear helmets. In states with no law or the latter one it is up to the rider and the passenger to determine what level of safety they are going to add to their riding experience.

Many riders do not like helmets, for a variety of reasons. They are hot in the summer. They can limit peripheral visibility. They impede hearing. They don't look cool. They are uncomfortable. They don't increase your chances of survival enough. Some of these reasons are valid and some are not. I have to admit I am guilty of not always wearing a helmet. Reasons one and four are my excuses. Most Harley riders and riders of other cruiser model motorcycles like to propagate the "biker image". It's hard to spend the weekend playing Jax Teller with your head all covered up with some un-cool looking helmet. And, by the way, the helmets that Jax and his Sons of Anarchy brothers wear in the show do not look to be DOT approved helmets. They appear to be too thin and light. The plain truth is that your chances of surviving an accident, or minimizing head trauma, are better with a helmet than without. And a helmet that is fitted correctly is hardly noticeable to the rider that he/she is wearing it. I have had two minor accidents and was wearing a helmet both times and was glad I was because I'm pretty sure my helmet made contact with the ground on both occasions.

In picking a helmet there are several things to consider. The very first thing is that it is a helmet that bears the seal of the Department of Transportation (DOT). The seal will be on the center back of the helmet down at the bottom. This means that the helmet has met or exceeded national safety standards and provides some adequate level of protection. Helmets without the DOT seal are considered worthless as far as protection goes, and are usually purchased for the "look" rather than the safety.

There are three different kinds of helmets: full-face, three-quarter, and half. The protection they offer decreases in the order listed. A full-face helmet offers, as the name suggests, protection to the entire face as well as the head and is, by far, the safest kind of helmet to be wearing. It usually comes with a face shield that tilts up and down and has protection around the jaw. You see them most on the riders of sports bikes. One reason is those bikes are faster, smaller, and usually performing the most hair-raising stunts on the road. Another reason is that helmet fits the sports bike image. Most riders of cruiser bikes don't like them for several of the reasons listed above. I do have to say though they are great in cold weather, when warmth means more than looking cool. Conversely, they can be uncomfortable in hot weather. I have friends that wear them in the winter and have another helmet for summer.

Three-quarter helmets completely cover the ears and usually come with a detachable face shield. Since it covers a little more of your head than the half helmet variety, it is a little safer than the half helmet, but much less safe than the full-face. For riders who want safety without having their entire face covered up, the three-quarter is a nice compromise.

The half helmet is for those riders trying to accomplish a good look and still maintaining some minimum level of safety. It stops just above the ears, but completely covers the top and sides of the head.

The next factor in selecting a helmet after you have decided on the kind you want is the fit. A helmet should fit snugly but not hurt your ears or head. To test the fit, put the helmet on and place your palms flat against each side of the helmet. Then try twisting your head back and forth. If your head moves inside the helmet more than a half an inch the helmet is too loose.

Another thing we were taught in the Riders Edge class was that if you drop your helmet from a height of two feet or more onto a hard surface you need to replace it. The impact can compromise the integrity of the shell's strength, making in unreliable in the event of an accident. For this reason it is recommended to never place your helmet on the seat of the bike or hang it from the handlebars. Some people hand it from the road pegs (the forward foot pegs) or the engine guard. Others take it with them when they leave the bike, guarding against helmet theft. If your bike has a tour box you can lock it in there.

Glasses and Goggles

Moving down from the head, let's talk about eyewear next. If you try riding with none you will quickly realize you need it simply so you can see. The same goes for the passenger. The wind will cause your eyes to tear up if you don't have something to buffer it. Plus there is a lot of dust and dirt swirling around out there and it will end up in your eyes. You will want the lenses to be shaded because your bike doesn't have a sun visor. Okay, so we need sunglasses. Not just any old pair of sunglasses, however. First, they need to be shatterproof. Second, you will want them to wrap around your head a little to minimize the amount of dirt that gets blown into your eyes. Third, they should also be a snug fit. You can buy motorcycle glasses or goggles just about anywhere. Goggles fit snugly on your face, have a foam liner to prevent wind and dirt from penetrating to your eyes, and have a strap to hold them in place. Purely from a protection standpoint, they are superior to sunglasses. They're the next best thing to a full-face helmet (which makes glasses as a wind buffer unnecessary due to the face shield). Goggles are also warmer in cold weather as they seal off the top of your face from the cold and biting wind. However, they are hot in warm weather and they have that un-cool stigma too. I keep a pair for winter riding. I used to use Oakley's for riding because they look cool, are shatterproof, and have wrap around models. Now I use a transitional pair of prescription eyeglasses so I can see near (my instrument panel) and far (the road). And, because they are transitional I don't need a different pair for night riding. You will, though. Have a second pair of glasses with clear lenses for nighttime.

Leather and Denim

It's not just for the look. Wearing leather and denim is like putting on an extra layer of skin…and the one you would want to leave on the pavement as opposed to the layers you were born with.

Denim and leather pants or chaps and jacket (especially in colder weather) will go along way towards avoiding cuts, scrapes and abrasions ("road rash"). This is the real reason bikers wear leather.

In warmer weather many bikers don't want to put on heavy leather. It's uncomfortable, especially when you are stopped and off your bike. There are some alternatives. Leather jackets come in different styles for different functions. The truly protective jackets are heavy and padded in places where you would need it. Some jackets even have removable plates in them for extra safety. Many leather jackets have an inside porous liner and two zippers. In warmer weather you can leave the outside zipper unzipped and just zip the liner zipper. This will allow air to pass through the liner and keep the rider cooler. Some jackets have removable liners. There are also lightweight leather jackets, which don't offer as much protection but are better than nothing. And, finally, there are denim jackets, which won't stand up to the asphalt as well as leather, but again, is better than most other kinds of outer wear.

You should also be aware that there are lines of biker clothes and boots that are "fashion" clothes and not designed for riding. Instead, they are designed to propagate the biker "look". They are great to wear to a rally or your favorite biker bar if you went in your cage. They offer little to nothing in the way of protection and safety. When buying riding clothes make sure they are approved for riding.

Leather pants or chaps are the best way to protect your legs, and to keep warm in the cooler weather. Leather pants are better because they completely cover the rider from the waist down, giving you more protection and warmth. Chaps look cooler though.

Nothing about riding is inexpensive, I've learned. You are going to pay a pretty price for quality leatherwear. But it is well worth the investment in terms of protection. Plus, quality leather items last a long time. Especially if you take care of them with a little bit of leather conditioner every once in awhile. My leathers are eight years old and look almost new.

Gloves

Next, we'll discuss the hands. There are two good reasons for wearing leather gloves at all times. The first, of course, is protection. If your bike goes down it is only natural to try to break the fall with your hands. Gloves will help to prevent you leaving your palms on the road.

The second reason is to prevent callouses from handlebar/grip vibration. On a short ride you won't notice the difference, but spend a few hours in the saddle without gloves and your hands will let you know they don't appreciate your inconsiderateness. In warmer weather I use the half-finger gloves. I wear out a pair every summer, so gloves are something that you might have to replace on a regular basis. Good pairs also have some palm padding in them for extra protection. If you get your gloves wet leave them out to air dry. I found out the hard way that throwing them into the saddlebag wet causes them to mildew and dry rot.

In colder weather I wear full-fingered gloves with a fur lining, for obvious reasons. The fit of your gloves, like everything else, is important. You don't want them too tight so that opening and clenching your hands is difficult or uncomfortable. You have to work your clutch and brake levers so you are going to be constantly flexing your grip. Make sure your gloves aren't an impediment to that.

I also have a pair of vortex gloves for bad/wet weather riding. They are super warm, but more important, unlike leather, they are waterproof. If I know I'm going to be riding in rain, rather than being surprised by it, I'll wear the vortex. If I am going to be riding in *really* cold weather, I'll wear the vortex. Otherwise, it's leather gloves, always.

Boots

The last protective item I want to talk about is boots. I'm not going to have much to say on this subject, but I want to impress upon you how important good, quality foot protection is. Again, it will not guarantee that you will not sustain an injury. But I can guarantee that the injury will be less severe if you are wearing boots as opposed to flip-flops or tennis shoes or some other kind of footwear that offers little to no protection. You can hurt your foot without ever dropping your bike. Feet, being the body part closest to the ground while riding (or doing anything other than standing on your head), can get injured by riding too close to a curb. If you do take a spill your bike can come down on your foot. You want good solid protection there.

Your boots should be made of leather and have a solid rubber sole. Leather soles slide too easily and you will be using your feet to hold your bike upright and back it up. You don't want your feet sliding out from under you.

The lace up kind of boot is safer than the slide-on type. In the event of an accident the lace-up kind won't come off your feet, leaving them exposed to injury. Steel toe is nice, but not absolutely necessary.

As mentioned before, there are fashion boots and riding boots. The fashion boots are not designed for riding and do not offer much in the way of protection. This is especially true for women. Remember, the passenger should be dressed as safely as the rider.

CHAPTER FIVE
RIDING AND THE LAWS OF PHYSICS

We are just going to talk about a few principles of physics that affect the behavior of your motorcycle and how to deal with them in this short chapter.

One of those principles is centrifugal force. This is the law that says when an object is traveling in a circle centrifugal force will pull the object to the outside edge of that circle. What this means to the rider of a motorcycle is that when you are going around a turn the bike will be pulled towards the outside of the turn. That means that, depending upon whether the turn is to the right or left, your bike is being pulled toward the centerline (and the oncoming lane of traffic) or the shoulder of the roadway (and the bar ditch just beyond). To combat this there is a proper way to ride through a turn. It is called outside-inside-outside.

Here is how it works. When approaching a significant turn in the roadway back off the throttle a little to slow down. Approach the turn from the outside of it. As you get further into the turn move the bike towards the inside of the turn and slightly accelerate. Lean through the turn keeping the bike under power (do not coast). As you get through the turn move the bike back towards the outside of the turn. This method minimizes the angle of the turn and lessens the effect of centrifugal force.

Going through a severe turn is one of the scarier things a new rider is asked to perform. You will do a lot of this during the safety class, but it will be at relatively slow speed, not highway speed. The rider's inclination is to try to go through the turn slowly, but this is a mistake. Remember our old adage that speed equals stability. The slower you are going the less stable the bike, and the last thing you want going through a turn is an unstable bike. Just like when in a cage, accelerating through the turn gives you more control of the vehicle. This is even truer on a motorcycle. If you go around a turn too slow I can guarantee that centrifugal force is going to pull you further to the outside of your turn. This is dangerous. A tight turn is made under power. I once had an experienced biker tell me that if you ever felt you were going to lose it on a turn (ride off the road), lean over as far as you can and give it full throttle. Those are the two factors that guard against the pull of centrifugal force. Leaning away from the force into the turn, and speed. Now I'm not saying to exceed the speed limit to get through a turn. This is one reason why you slow before entering the turn, so that you can accelerate back to highway speed as you go through it.

You have seen the diamond-shaped yellow road advisory signs that will tell you in advance about a turn in the road way and which direction the turn takes. Underneath the sign will be posted the speed in which to go through the turn safely. If there is no speed posted that means you can proceed through the turn at the road's speed limit. The more severe the angle of the turn, the lower the posted speed will be. If you encounter such a sign that says you have a turn to the left coming up and posts a 35 mph safe speed, slow to 35 or less as you enter the turn from the right side of the road. Then drop down to the inside of the turn by leaning and moving left while accelerating the bike by about 5-10 mph. Come out of the turn by moving back to the right as you approach the straightaway.

The biggest reason for single motorcycle accidents (accidents not involving another vehicle) is taking a turn at too great a speed and failing to hold it. If you are unfamiliar with a road it is wise to ride it more slowly and cautiously then one you are familiar with. Turns have a bad habit of sneaking up on you if you are not paying close attention, and sometimes even if you are because many of them are not marked with a caution sign as they should be.

I have mentioned that speed equals stability several times. Obviously, the opposite is true as well. A stationary bike is the least stable. Imagine standing a bike up without its kickstand down and letting go of it. Where is it going? Over. When a bike is not moving it is more subject to the forces of gravity. The slower you are riding the greater the gravitational pull on the bike. Motorcycles are built with balance in mind, and no matter how heavy a bike looks (or is) they are not difficult to hold in an upright position. However, the heavier the bike the less you can let it lean to one side or the other when standing still. You will not be able to hold up a heavy bike if you tip it more than a few degrees left or right. A light bike can be tipped a much greater distance and you can still bring it back up to 90 degrees vertical without much effort.

If you see a bike wobble as it is approaching a stop, or leaving one, that is usually an indicator that the rider is still inexperienced. Once you have become familiar with your bike's "feel" and have learned how to use the throttle, clutch and brakes for smooth stops and starts, you won't wobble your bike when slowing to a stop or starting off from one. The wobble is due to the forces of gravity trying to wrest control of the bike from the rider.

In summary, just remember that, contrary to your instincts, speed and leaning the bike while under power are your best weapons against the laws of physics. Practicing these things in a parking lot will make clear what I am talking about. Set up a course of cones and try riding through them without getting outside the cones. You will quickly notice you are better able to stay within the course and keep your turns tighter when you slightly accelerate the bike rather than letting it coast. This is exponentially true when out on the highway.

CHAPTER SIX
DEFENSIVE RIDING

You may have heard the expression "Loud Pipes Saves Lives". What this expression means is that if other drivers know where you are there is less chance that they will run over you or run you off the road. Now, I am not advocating for loud pipes. I am, however, advocating for letting drivers of four wheeled vehicles now where you are at all times. There are a number of ways to do this and we will discuss them in this, the most important chapter in the book.

One of the urban myths out there regarding motorcycle riding is that most bike accidents are the fault of the driver of the car or truck, and not the rider of the motorcycle. However, statistics do not support this hypothesis. Fully fifty percent of accidents involving a motorcycle and some other kind of vehicle were the fault of the motorcycle rider.

Defensive riding on a motorcycle is the most important thing you need to learn and practice to increase your chances of having a trouble-free ride. You may have had occasion to take a Defensive Driving Course for motorists at some point during your driving years. These same principles apply tenfold to riding a motorcycle. And for the same reason I have already mentioned several times earlier in this book. An accident on a motorcycle is much more likely to cause bodily harm than if you are in a car or truck (cage).

In this chapter I plan to discuss three main themes. The first is the one mentioned above, making sure other drivers know where you are. The second is proper lane positioning for optimum safety. The third is "intuitive riding", a term I made up myself but basically means being able to anticipate what other vehicles are going to do, or may do, before they do it.

So lets begin with letting other drivers know where you are. Loud pipes aside, some motorcycles are easy to hear and some are not. But for a cage driver with the windows rolled up and the radio on, sometimes even the loudest of bikes go unheard. So there are some additional things you can do to ensure that drivers know where you are. Most of these will be obvious; the trick is putting them into practice on the road. And all of these can be practiced when you are driving a cage as well as your bike.

Your motorcycle's headlight is always on for a reason. That reason is so that other drivers can more easily see you. I remember when the law requiring motorcycle headlights to be on whenever the bike is being operated was passed. Before then there were on/off switches for your headlight(s). After that law was passed headlights came on and turned off with the ignition switch. There is a belief that sometimes drivers of cages do not "see" motorcycles like they do other cages, and also don't do a good job of gauging their speed relative to other vehicles on the roadway. The headlight law was enacted to counteract those beliefs. Your bike's manufacturer has taken care of this little safety item for you. Now let's discuss what you can do to minimize your chances of a mishap on the highway.

Blind Spots

The first is staying out of a driver's "blind spot". Seems obvious, right? But the fact is that if you are just rolling along with traffic and not really paying attention it is easy to fall into the blind spot of the vehicle ahead of you that is in an adjacent lane. Always be aware of where you are in relation to other vehicles…and where other vehicles are in relation to you. This second item is important because it may become necessary for you to make an evasive maneuver in order to avoid a vehicle whose driver did not see you and moved into your lane, forcing you to take action to avoid a collision. You don't want to jump "from the frying pan into the fire" so to speak. You need to know what your escape routes are and you can only know that by knowing where other traffic is. As far as blind spots go, just remember that if you can look in a cage's side mirrors and see the driver, then he/she can see you too.

Maintain Your Safety Cushion

I always thought that riders who tailgated cars or trucks were among the stupidest of God's creatures. While it is true that a motorcycle requires less stopping distance than a cage, you still do not want to be put in the position of having to slam your brakes on at 70 mph to avoid becoming a squashed insect on the back door of an eighteen wheeler. Always maintain at least a two second following distance behind the vehicle ahead of you. I always try to maintain at least that much distance to avoid emergency braking situations. When the brake lights of the vehicle in front of me come on I immediately release the throttle and prepare to brake if I need to. Another practice of mine is to try not to ride behind high-profile vehicles. This prevents me from being able to see the traffic ahead and anticipate when the vehicle directly in front of me might start to brake. I like to be able to see several vehicles ahead of me so I can slow down before it becomes necessary to brake. I will usually change lanes to avoid being behind these types of vehicles. However, it is not always possible to avoid being behind a vehicle that restricts your visibility, so when I am behind a high-profile vehicle, and this can even be a pickup or SUV, I increase my safety cushion to three of four seconds to give me more room to stop or change lanes to avoid a wreck.

Use Your Horn

Here is another obvious one. Don't save your horn for when a vehicle is already in the process of making a move that puts you in danger. If you think a driver is unaware of your presence, give a toot on your horn to let him know you are there. If they don't like the fact that you beeped your horn at them, too bad. It is better to be safe than to be sorry. This goes for other motorcycles too. I frequently check my mirrors (also an important defensive riding technique) but I am still amazed how many times another bike zooms past me that I never knew was there. If you are going to pass another rider and you have not received any indication that he knows you are there give your horn a tap before going by him. Bikers usually perceive this as a friendly hello anyway. The problem with motorcycle horns are that most of them sound like toys, and are not audible to drivers inside of vehicles with windows rolled up. I have always been amazed by the fact that bikes are not equipped with horns equal to car horns. I don't know what the rationale is, but when you need one they often are ineffective because of their low decibels. For that reason I fitted my bike with an air horn that is about five times louder than my stock horn. A driver wearing Bose headphones and blasting himself with Metallica can hear this horn.

Make Eye Contact

A very effective way of ensuring that a motorist sees you is simply making eye contact. This is especially effective when facing each other at an intersection. If you are stopped at a traffic light waiting for it to turn green and across the intersection is a vehicle wanting to turn left across your path, making eye contact with him or her ensures that they see you and won't cut in front of you. If you are looking at them and are unable to make eye contact, try revving your engine, waving, or giving a toot on your horn. If they still don't look at you it is time to become a little alarmed that they are not as focused on their driving as they need to be. When the light turns green, proceed through the intersection only after you have satisfied yourself that the vehicle in question is going to wait until you've gone by.

Now let's talk about lane positioning. As a rider of a motorcycle you have, unlike a cage, the option of three different positions within your lane. You can choose to ride on the left side (where a car's left tires would be), the middle of the lane, or the right side. Different situations dictate where you position the bike among those three choices.

One unwritten rule regarding lane positioning is, "don't encourage a driver to share your lane." Since a motorcycle takes up only a third of a lane and if you are over on the far left, a driver to your right may be encouraged to move into your lane adjacent to you to get around a slower vehicle in front of him. This puts you in danger. Therefore, whenever you are riding in the far left hand lane (the "speed" lane) of a multi-lane highway, stay to the right side of the lane (where a car's right side tires would be). This discourages a cage from floating over into your lane, pressing you towards the left shoulder. Conversely, if you are riding in the far right hand lane (the "slow" lane), stay to the left side of your lane to prevent a car floating over from your left into your lane.

I like to use the middle of my lane during wet weather. The crown of the road, plus the depressed asphalt in the tracks of where the tires of four-wheeled vehicles ride, causes the middle lane position to be the driest because it is higher than the right or left sides.

I always like to use the far left lane, or "speed" lane, for riding because I only have to worry about traffic to the right of me encroaching on my space, plus there is a shoulder on my left for breakdowns or emergencies. However, if you are going to ride in that lane you need to make sure you maintain a speed that does not slow the traffic in that lane. If you are not comfortable riding at that speed move over a lane to your right and ride the speed limit.

When selecting what lane position you want to ride in, be cognizant of where the blind spots are for the drivers around you. If you select a lane position that makes it hard for a driver ahead of you to see you in his mirror then you need to make an adjustment.

The last thing I want to talk about in this chapter is what I call "intuitive riding". This simply means quickly processing the positions and speeds of the vehicles around you and recognizing what certain vehicles might do if certain situations arise. This is the critical part of defensive riding. The longer that you have been driving a cage the easier this will be for you to do, based on having experienced, at one time or another, just about every possible scenario on a roadway. The difference is on a motorcycle you need to be hyper-vigilant in this regard as you are at a safety disadvantage simply by being on a motorcycle.

This also pertains to vehicles that might pull out into the roadway in front of you. One of the reasons that I feel freeway riding is safer than riding on city streets is all of the unknown variables presented on city streets by cars pulling out of parking lots, driveways or side streets onto the roadway. Another is the constant changing of lanes by vehicles to try to gain a forward progress advantage. These lane changes are often made with little thought and no preparation, such as checking mirrors or using a turn signal. It's a last minute decision and can be a disastrous one for you on a motorcycle. Always be aware of the traffic up ahead, either on the road or getting ready to enter it.

Riding intuitively simply means using all of your experience as a motor vehicle operator constantly. It's a good practice to use all of the time, but we all know that when driving a car we often spend our time deep in thought about things other than driving. On a motorcycle this can get you killed rather easily.

There is a reason Defensive Driving courses are taught for drivers found to be in violation of the traffic laws, and a reason why auto insurance companies will give premium discounts to drivers that have completed one. The intent of these courses is to make you a more vigilant and cautious driver. A more vigilant and cautious driver has a greatly improved chance of not being in an accident. That's the category you want to be in when riding a motorcycle.

CHAPTER SEVEN
RIDING EXPERIENCE

Most bikers measure rider experience in terms of how many years they have ridden. I do not think this is the best way to gauge experience, but for our purposes here it will serve. Later in the chapter we will discuss another, more accurate, way of determining the experience of a rider. We will also talk about what a rider is experienced enough to attempt and what he/she is not.

A rider's skillset and confidence grows with experience. We are going to breakdown length of experience into categories and discuss some of the rider's traits in those two areas (skillset and confidence) within those categories.

First Six Months

During a rider's first six months time should be spent practicing what was learned during the safety course. That means starting out in parking lots and neighborhood streets. Confidence and skillset are low at this point, but practice can help to improve both dramatically. For one thing you will become much more familiar with your motorcycle. Learning how it handles, accelerates, and stops are essential pieces of knowledge for when you are on the highway. In a large parking lot you should be practicing starts, stops, and turns. You should be learning to master your bike at slow speeds, which, you will recall, is when the bike is least stable. You should be learning how to accelerate through turns, and working on making your turns tighter each practice session.

Work on lining your bike up at a parking space and backing the bike into the center of the parking slot. The harder part is not pushing your bike backwards but turning the front end away from the space so that the bike ends up directly in front of the position you want to park it in. You will usually want to park your bike facing out into the roadway so that you don't have to push it back into traffic. But, you also don't want to try to push your bike backwards on an incline. Always have your front wheel on the high side of an incline, unless your bike comes equipped with reverse (which very few do). This means that sometimes you will be parked facing away from the traffic flow, but backing down an incline is easier and is accomplished rather quickly. This is not as important if you have a very light bike, but with a cruiser this can mean the difference between a quick exit and having to ask someone to help you push your bike out of its parking space. Remember, if parking on an incline, roll in and power out. When parallel parking do not park your bike parallel to the curb like you would a car. This invites a motorist to "share" your parking space should there be a shortage of them, thereby penning you in. Always park at an angle so that you take up the majority of the width of the space. Face the bike slightly towards the direction you will be leaving if you backed in; or slightly away from the direction you will be leaving if you pulled in front first.

In addition to parking lot practice you should be riding around your neighborhood and practicing starts and stops at all the stop signs, slow turns on residential streets, and begin interacting with other traffic. It is normal to be a little nervous but this is essential for getting you ready for the open road. You may drop your bike at an intersection, or feel that you don't have total control of it as you stop. This is normal and is why you are practicing. With each session you will get better and your confidence will grow.

From neighborhood streets I moved on to rural roads as I lived out in the country and that is what we had. These roads can be a little more dangerous than a state or interstate highway as they are often two lanes with some intermittent passing lanes and often no shoulders and no turn lanes. They also will have more radical turns and steeper hills, which, of course, make them a blast to ride. As far as accidents go, there are less of them on rural roadways but the mortality rate is higher, largely due to the slower response time of emergency vehicles. Also wildlife, particularly deer, can pose a very real problem. You must watch out for them just as you would watch out for other vehicles on the roadway.

When I was taking the rider safety course I made myself three promises, all of which I broke within the first couple of months. I promised I would not ride faster than 60 mph, I would not ride on interstate highways, and I would not ride in cities. These were ridiculous promises and were an indication of my over-cautious mindset. If you never break 60 mph you are going to get pushed off the highway. I found interstate highways among the safest (and most boring) rides. You cannot avoid cities if you are going to spend anytime at all on a motorcycle. City riding is, indeed, higher risk, but if you follow good defensive riding techniques you will minimize the chances of mishap.

After a month of practicing in parking lots, neighborhoods, and rural roadways I felt ready for the main roads and higher traffic volumes.

Second Six Months

About the time I was finishing up my first six months as a rider I had a very experienced rider tell me the second six months were often the most dangerous because your confidence grew faster than your skill level did. In other words, you thought you could do more than you could actually, and safely, do. This turned out to be prophetic for me as shortly after that conversation I failed to negotiate a turn, hit a curb and took a spill that damaged my bike to the tune of $13,000 and caused my ex-wife to be airlifted to a hospital and undergo neck surgery. So all I'm going to say about the second six months is that you need to continue to use this period of time as a learning process, improving your skills and becoming more aware of things that can happen on the roadways. Stay alert and always respect the bike and know what it can do and what it cannot do; and what YOU can do and cannot do.

I have advocated caution throughout this and previous chapters, but I do not want to convey the feeling that you should ride in fear. The exact opposite is true, as riding is one of the most pleasurable experiences you will have, I am sure. Riding with confidence is the safest way to ride, as long as that confidence is based on your knowledge and your developing skillset, and not on some imaginary fantasy of you as Evel Knievel.

One Year

After a year of riding, and I mean at least 10,000 miles logged during that year, you are experienced enough to try two more activities. The first is riding two-up and the second is group riding. Now this may sound foolish to you, and I didn't wait a year to do either, although the information I read cautioned me to…and I wish I had. The accident I mentioned above occurred while I was riding two-up and was a direct result of group riding. Today I would not have that accident. I would negotiate that turn easily without a second thought. My inexperience and nervousness at riding with a group that was riding faster than I was comfortable with caused me to miss that turn. Had I not been riding two-up no one would have been hurt as I ended up only suffering a scraped knuckle.

Foolish as it may sound, you should not do either of these things until you've gained enough experience to do them without worry. The dynamics of the bike change when a passenger is added to the equation. And group riding has certain rules to follow that we will discuss later in the book.

Let's talk here a little bit about riding two-up. Adding a passenger adds weight to the bike and changes the distribution of the weight. This is not necessarily a bad thing since it puts that weight directly over the rear wheel, increasing traction. But it does take a little getting used to, especially on starts and stops. Until you and your passenger develop some experience and get into sync with one another, stopping the bike under full control can be a little tricky. Also, adding a passenger changes the balance of the bike and the physics involved in keeping it upright. The passenger has to remember to sit still when the bike is moving slowly or is stopped. Every movement of the passenger creates movement of the bike, and, for the rider, it is usually an unexpected movement. When the bike is traveling at highway speed the rider can barely even tell the passenger is back there, but when traveling slowly it is very apparent that someone is on the back and that someone can affect the bike's handling. Additionally, when going through turns the passenger needs to lean as the rider does, no more and no less.

Also, a passenger should never get on or off the bike until the rider tells him/her that he is ready for them to do so. It is the rider's job to hold the bike upright while the passenger mounts and dismounts. That means the rider has to be standing up, straddling the bike with both feet firmly on the ground. The passenger, once she has started to mount or dismount, needs to complete the move quickly.

Miles vs. Time

At the beginning of this chapter I talked about a better way to measure rider experience. When a rider says he or she has been riding for a year you may make certain assumptions about their skill level over someone who says they have been riding for five years. However, everyone rides a different amount of miles per year. That person who has ridden only a year may have logged 25,000 miles during that year, while the other rider may be doing 5,000 a year. That would put them at equal experience (25,000 miles). I have seen 5 or 6 year old bikes for sale that look brand new and then notice that they don't even have 10,000 miles on them.

I have been riding for 8 years at the time of this writing, and I have logged 91,000 miles on a motorcycle up to now. That's not a gargantuan amount, but it comes out to 11,375 a year, and that is more than a lot of riders who have been riding for that same amount of time. Sometimes you will hear someone say they have been riding for 20+ years, but then you learn they rode for about 5 years then stopped riding for 15 years and then picked it up again. That rider doesn't have 20+ years experience, he has 5+. And he's rusty!

So keep track of your mileage. It's easy to do. I have had two bikes. I put 11,500+ miles on the Road King, and 79,000+ miles on the Electra Glide. I probably have put about 500 miles on two other bikes we have owned at one time or another as well. I have ridden from Austin, Texas to Las Vegas, Nevada; to Colorado; to New Mexico twice, and to Florida twice. I have also ridden all over the state of Texas and took a trip through Louisiana and Arkansas. I have many more trips I want to take. I want to ride in the Pacific

Northwest and also in Montana, Idaho, and the Dakotas. I want to ride in the Blue Ridge Mountains. I plan to do all of these things at one time or another. I never have trailered my bike anywhere because for me it is never about the destination, but about the trip getting there and getting home. I love to ride and I can do it all day.

People always ask me if I have been to Sturgis. Well, I have, but not for a motorcycle rally. I was there in 1968 when two buddies and I drove from New York to Wyoming and back during the summer of that year. Sturgis, South Dakota, surrounded by the Black Hills, held its first rally in 1938. It's great riding country, although I have yet to do it. Back in 1968 I had never heard of Sturgis or the rally. We blew through the town and that was that. Those early rallies were held largely for motorcycle racing and stunt riding. That very first rally back in 1938 was created by Pappy Hoel of the Jackpine Gypsies Motorcycle Club (MC) and was called The Black Hills Classic according to Wikipedia. Pappy also owned an Indian Motorcycle Dealership in Sturgis that he opened that same year.

I am not a Rally guy. I much prefer to spend my time riding than sitting around some Rally site with thousands of other bikers. But there is no denying that they are indeed popular among millions of bikers nationwide. The Sturgis Rally alone will bring in $800+ million to the economy of southern South Dakota this year.

CHAPTER EIGHT
BAD WEATHER RIDING

When I speak of "bad" weather, I mean inclement weather, not cold weather, which the proper clothing takes care of. Unless we are talking ice, then cold weather also becomes inclement weather. So, the kinds of weather we are talking about are:

> ➤ rain
> ➤ snow
> ➤ fog
> ➤ wind
> ➤ ice

Always know what the weather is going to be wherever you plan to be riding. Make sure you have a good weather source available to you at all times. Usually a good phone app will do the trick. If you know what the weather will be you can decide whether it is worth riding that day or not, but at the very least you can be prepared for the weather as far as clothing goes. For cold weather it is best to dress in layers, allowing you to remove clothing should temperatures warm up.

Let's talk about rain first. Other than wind, rain is the most common condition you are likely to encounter on a motorcycle. Most people think the worst aspect of rain is reduced traction, in addition to riding soaked and uncomfortable, but it really is reduced visibility. The problem is, in addition to the normal limited visibility caused by a hard rain, the fact that your goggles and your windshield are covered with water and no real way to keep them clear. This vastly decreases your ability to see. And the smallness of your bike compared to other vehicles on the road reduces your ability to be seen.

Your first precaution against rain is having good quality rain gear. I don't mean ponchos designed for campers, which the wind will shred off your body like so many garbage bags, but rain gear designed for motorcycle riding. These can be purchased at most motorcycle dealerships. I bought my first and second set from Harley-Davidson. They not only keep you completely dry, but warm too. The jacket can be worn in dry, cooler weather and it is reflective as well so that you are more easily seen by other motorists. My first set of rain gear blew off the back of my bike where it was secured poorly after having removed it following a short rainstorm in West Texas. Not wanting to stow it away wet, I draped it over my luggage and tucked it under the tie downs, believing that would hold it in place. I was wrong. Somewhere around the Balmorhea exit of I-10 it blew away. There went one hundred and fifty dollars, gone with the wind. I picked up a second set in Phoenix, Arizona on that same trip. The gear is always on my bike because you just never know when it is going to be needed.

Your second precaution is to treat your windshield and your goggles with a water repellant product such as Rain-X. This helps to shed water off of these surfaces rather than leaving big, hard-to-see-through raindrops.

You must be extra vigilant about your positioning so that you are not in the blind spots of other drivers. Remember the trick about riding the middle of the lane for keeping less water under your tires. And slow down. You see the signs "Slow Down on Wet Roads" all the time. Well, it's even more imperative on a two-wheeled vehicle. A hydroplaning motorcycle is no fun at all. Remember that metal surfaces, such as cattle guards, manhole covers, and some bridge surfaces, are slipperier when wet than the normal road surface. Be extra cautious on these. Slower speed and an even controlled throttle are important, as is smooth, slow braking.

Another thing to avoid is high water crossings. Cars and trucks are no match against rushing water. Much less of it is needed to push a motorcycle downriver. Also remember when crossing water on the roadway, whether raining or not, the bottom surface can be slick with algae. It is best to power the bike before hitting the water and then coasting through it to keep your rear wheel from spinning out. Keep your feet up if you are not wearing rain pants because the bike is going to splash water onto your legs as you cross through it.

Living in Texas I do not have much experience riding in snow. I have ridden in some snow in the Colorado Mountains, but for the most part the roadways were clear and dry. This is your main concern. There is nothing to worry about riding in snow if the roadways are clear. If they are not, stay off them. That's my advice. The only other hazard snow presents is one of visibility, and it is not as big a hazard as rain presents in that department. Snow flurries are barely noticeable. Heavier snow presents some visibility problems and worsening road condition problems. It is best to be avoided.

Fog, like snow, is best to be avoided as well. Riding in fog presents the same danger that driving a car in fog presents…that being one of visibility. If you get caught in fog and have no choice but to ride, then slow down and stay to the right. A motorcycle is likely to be less visible than a car and there is always a danger of someone hitting you from behind. In the right hand lane you will be traveling with the slower traffic and have an accessible escape route if need be. Keep your headlights on low beam. As soon as possible get off the roadway and wait out the fog in a safe place. Fog is usually a fairly short-term condition and it is better to wait and be late than risk being killed.

Wind is an extremely common condition for riders and learning how to handle it is not difficult. Fifty percent of the time the wind will be hitting you broadside, which, of course, is more dangerous in terms of affecting your bike than a head or tail wind. There are two things to remember when riding in wind. Lean into the wind and speed equals stability. The bike is less susceptible to counter-balance forces at a higher rate of speed than a slower rate. Slowing down in windy conditions puts you at greater risk than maintaining highway speed. If the wind is hitting you from the right side, lean the bike slightly right to counter the wind's effect. I once rode a couple hundred miles along Texas' Gulf coast with my son and son-in-law with a hellacious wind coming off the water and blasting us from the east as we rode north. We were leaning our bikes right for all we were worth and that just kept them upright at a

90 degree angle. The wind constantly tried to blow us into the adjacent lane so we stayed in the farthest right hand lane so that there was plenty of road to our left. It was raining for most of that trip too which made it extra stressful, but didn't change the dynamics too much. Stay right, lean right, and maintain speed. Of course, I would hope it goes without saying, the process is reversed if the wind is coming from your left.

Ice....stay home...period. There is nothing more helpless than being at the wheel of a car that is skidding out of control on an icy road...unless that is being on a motorcycle in the same condition. The bike is going down, period. If you are riding along and encounter icy conditions, get off the road. There is no skill for circumventing ice on a roadway. Plus a car skidding towards you out of control is a rather scary sight as well...best to be avoided.

This brings me to a brief discussion about riding on poor road surfaces, regardless of weather. Don't we wish all roadways could be nice smooth asphalt or concrete? But they are not. I do my best to avoid roads that are not, simply because my Harley is not a dirt bike. If you are riding an off-road bike then any kind of road surface usually presents an enjoyable challenge. If you are on a cruiser, well, they like the main road. You definitely want to avoid gravel roads, and gravel on a road, whenever you can. The bike has virtually no stability on gravel and neither do you when you put your feet down to hold the bike up. Roads with lots of potholes make for interesting riding as well. You have to keep all your focus on avoiding dropping your front wheel into a chuckhole and flipping back end over front in which is bound to be an ugly and expensive spill. I don't like dirt roads either, even if it is road base material. Dirt roads usually bring along the problems of slippery material, poor traction, dust, and potholes. They also can be muddy if there has been a recent rain. None of these things are good.

CHAPTER NINE
RIDING CLUBS AND ORGANIZATIONS

Personally, I like to ride alone or with one or two other guys. I have belonged to two riding groups, and there is no denying that the camaraderie and friendships gained are terrific. But essentially, being a little bit of a control freak, I like to be in control of my route, pace, and itinerary on any given ride. I like to be in charge of deciding where and how long I am going to stop and how many miles I'm going to ride that day. When riding in a group you give up that control to someone else. But group riding is a tremendous experience, and one you should experience, as it will make you a better rider.

There are essentially three different kinds of riding groups that I am going to categorize as:

1. Riding Clubs
2. Non-Profit Motorcycle Organizations
3. Motorcycle Clubs (MC's)

There are all kinds of riding clubs, and their main mission is to get out on motorcycles and enjoy the road. One of the biggest is the Harley Owners' Group (HOG), and every dealership has a chapter. There are riding clubs centered around the type of motorcycle you ride, around military affiliations, around public servant affiliation, around religious affiliations, etc. The HOG groups are an example of the first one. The Leathernecks are an example of the second and is made up of current and former U.S. Marines. There are also a lot of veterans groups. The Blue Knights are made up of law enforcement officers. There are numerous examples of the last, most are Christian groups such as Riders for Jesus. There is the Patriot Guard, which escorts and attends the funerals of fallen soldiers. Most, if not all, of these groups engage in charity events to raise funds for good causes and they do this through activities that involve motorcycle riding, such as Toy Runs or Poker Runs or Motorcycle Rallies.

Non-profit motorcycle organizations exist for the purpose of providing help or support in an area that qualifies for an exemption under the IRS tax code. The two that I belonged to were Bikers Against Child Abuse (BACA) and Guardians of the Children (GOC). As the names suggest, these organizations provided help, support, and protection to abused children, usually while going through the legal system with a prosecution of the alleged offender. I was a patched member of both and enjoyed the experience related to the mission. I made many friends that I still call "brother" today. I would recommend either of these two fine organizations to the rider who wants to do something a little more meaningful with his/her time on a motorcycle.

MC's are the organizations that have the "bad boy" image. Some deserved, some not. Serving in BACA and GOC I came across many MCs and MC members, albeit on a superficial basis, like participating in fundraisers, rallies, or representing my organization at a Meeting of Clubs, which included all three of the riding clubs listed above.

Probably the two best-known MC's are the Hell's Angels and the Bandido's. There is no doubt that the activities of these two groups, and many more like them, have been suspect and criminal at times, but they also have done many good works as well. These MC's are made up of bikers who call themselves "ten percenters". Many years ago, when MC's were springing up in the 1940's and 50's, there was concern among motorcycle manufacturers that motorcycles and motorcycle riding would get a bad image from these clubs. So, Harley Davidson put out an ad that stated that 90% of all motorcycle riders were honest, law-abiding citizens like you and me that simply enjoyed the thrill of riding motorcycles. This prompted the MC's to adopt the term "ten percenters" as they fell outside the 90% identified by H-D. If you look at an MC member's vest you may see a diamond shaped patch that say "10%". That is what it stands for. The intimidating image of motorcycle clubs is not one that is discouraged by MC's. In fact, it is part of their persona and they propagate it well.

In the world of MC's they have their own set of unwritten rules and forms of etiquette. If you are not aware of these it is easy to commit an unintended transgression and that may have unpleasant consequences. The advice I received, and always adhered to, when I rode with BACA was not to talk or interact with MC members unless one speaks to you. And then always be respectful and don't try to be too familiar. Do not call one "brother" or the diminutive "bro". If you are not in his club you are not his "brother".

So these are the three different kinds of riding clubs. All have different missions and objectives and attract different kinds of riders. Unfortunately, to the uneducated, all fall into the public perception of MC's, but, as you can see, this is not the case. All three groups usually wear vests and patches (colors), but unless you know the difference you are likely to think of them as all the same.

One way you can tell an MC from the other two groups are MC patches will be a combination of two patches, while the others will be single patches. MC patches will have the club patch, and then below it will be a separate chapter patch. Riding Clubs and non-profit organizations will have all of that information on a single patch.

In all MC's that I am aware of patches have to be "earned". Until a member "earns" his patch he is a "prospect". In the two non-profit riding organizations I was a member of patches also had to be "earned". This was accomplished by a certain amount of time riding with the group and a certain level of activity/participation. Earning your patch is a very proud moment and wearing your colors is a true badge of honor to the member and his/her brothers and sisters.

There are a few unwritten rules around wearing your colors. You never wear them in a cage. Take them off and lay them on the back seat or put them in the trunk. Never leave your colors unattended in public. I learned this lesson the hard way. Right after I got patched I wore my colors to a BACA event at a junior high school football game in which on of our BACA kids was playing. Our president decided that perhaps wearing our colors might not be a good idea as most people did not know the young man had been sexually abused, so he had us take them off and fold them up. Later I went down to the concession stand to get something to eat and when I returned my vest was gone. I immediately noticed but no one would tell me where it was. At the end of the game our president returned it to me with the admonishment that I never, ever leave my vest. If I have to take it off then give it to another member to hold until I get back. He said if an MC member saw my colors unattended he would take it and I would never get it back. Also, clubs riding outside their own area have to secure permission from the local reigning MC (in Texas usually the Bandidos) to wear their colors through their area. It seems stupid I know, but it is their rules and it is best to follow them than defy them.

No matter what kind of riding club you belong to, you will have one thing in common. You will be doing "group riding". Group riding looks simple, but in fact, it is a learned art. And something you shouldn't attempt until you have at least 10,000 miles logged on a motorcycle.

There is no doubt that a long line of bikers cruising down the highway is an impressive and attention-getting phenomenon. Who would not want to be a part of that? I loved it. But it made me nervous too as I was too inexperienced a rider to be trying to keep up with the skill level of guys who had been riding for many years. The speed was often faster than I was comfortable with and it was hard for me to maintain proper spacing until I had been doing it for about six months.

When riding in a group there are a few "do's" and "don'ts you need to be aware of. Unlike the way Hollywood likes to depict group riding, you never ride next to another rider. You stagger the two lines so each rider has the whole lane if needed and one rider doesn't drift into another rider. You maintain a two second interval from the bike in front of you. No less than that or you are too close and no more than that or the gap between riders becomes large enough for a car to squeeze in and break up the group. Large groups should break up into smaller groups of five or six bikes as it is easier to stay together and to make lane changes, and it is also more considerate to other motorists. However, a lot of times they do not do that. Your two best riders should be lead and "tail gunner" or "sweeper" (last in line). Each has a critical role. The lead rider decides on lane changes and when and where to pass slower vehicles. The last rider seals off the lane that the group is moving into so that the group can move as one. The last rider is also responsible for stopping with any bikes that breakdown or have an accident. The rest of the group continues on until reaching a safe stopping point and waits on the other bikes. If you are in touch by cell phone you can make a plan to deal with the incident. If not, one rider with decision-making authority should return to the scene of the incident.

Once you become proficient at group riding you will see that it is a safer way to ride as larger groups are easy to see and motorists usually steer clear of them. Keeping to the speed limit insures that no one in the group is going to get a speeding ticket. Finally, there is always help available if needed.

For any group going on a lengthy ride it is helpful to have a person who determines the meet spot and pre-arranged stopping places along the route that he has planned in advance. In most clubs this person is called the Road Captain. The Road Captain shares this information with the group before the ride begins so that they know the route and the stopping points. The Road Captain should also have at least one alternative route in mind in case of unforeseen circumstances such as accidents, traffic jams, road construction, etc.

In summary, belonging to a riding club is a great experience. You will build your motorcycle knowledge from interacting with others and you will develop some life-long friendships.

One other thing I want to mention. All bikers form a "brotherhood" of sorts. We wave to each other when passing. We visit with each other when stopped at rest areas or gas stations/convenience stores. We stop to offer help if we encounter one stopped on the side of the road. We do this because we share a passion for the activity and an elevated risk level to indulge that passion, and we appreciate each other for it. If you do decide to become a rider, join the "brotherhood".

CHAPTER TEN
SERVICE AND MAINTENANCE

The care and feeding of your motorcycle is of utmost importance. As you have no doubt noticed, I never tire of telling you that your life is often in the hands of your motorcycle. And keeping that in mind, I always want to be on a motorcycle that has the least chance of failing me mechanically. My bike is eight years old and there is always a good chance of something going wrong while on a ride. As a result, I take every precaution to make sure everything is in good working order, that my bike is well maintained, and that my tires have plenty of tread.

The first thing you can do in this regard is to give your bike a quick walk-around check before every ride. I always check my tires because a tire is the one thing I least want to have a problem with while speeding down the highway. If you blowout a tire at 70 mph, especially the front one, keeping the bike upright until you come to a stop will be a real challenge of your skill and a real test of your luck as far as how close other vehicles are to you. I check the tires for tread wear, inflation, and making sure there are no missing chunks of rubber. I also check for any fluid leaks of any kind, both on the ground and on any engine parts. I make sure my horn and all my lights and turn directionals work. Upon starting the bike I listen to how the engine starts and sounds. You will become very familiar with what your bike normally sounds like, and any deviation from that sound usually indicates a problem. Also, you can tell if your battery is still doing an adequate job of turning over the engine. Every couple of months I take a wrench and make sure all the bolts are tight. Engine vibration can loosen bolts no matter how well torqued they are. When I do this I also check my inspection sticker to see when my next inspection is due. It is not as obvious on motorcycles as it is on cars and I have trouble remembering what month the last one was done.

The next thing I do is take the bike in for service every 5,000 miles. As long as your bike is on warranty, and especially if you purchased a service plan, use your dealership. Not only do they do the obvious things, they check everything and most of those things you wouldn't know how to check or have the proper tools or instruments to do it right. They also have the parts available (usually) if replacements are needed. This may be a little more expensive, but isn't your life and well being worth it? If you can't afford the service then you can't afford the motorcycle. Since my bike went off warranty I have used independent shops or mechanics occasionally, but they are always Harley-Davidson certified mechanics.

I use premium gasoline and synthetic oil in my motorcycle. The premium gasoline is recommended by the manufacturer and if I'm only putting 4+ gallons in at a time the price difference isn't going to break me....but the price of a new engine might. The synthetic oil is not necessarily recommended and any premium regular oil will do just fine. I use synthetic oil because the viscosity won't beak down until 7,500-10,000 miles, giving me a safe cushion between oil changes. It's a little more expensive, but worth it to me. Motorcycles generally sit longer between starts than cars and trucks do, so I want good quality fluids inside my engine that I know I can count on to do the job they are designed to do.

I replace my tires according to a regular schedule. My front tire gets replaced every 10,000-15,000 miles and my rear tire every 15,000-20,000 miles, unless tire wear indicates changing them sooner than that. Again, a blowout in a four-wheel vehicle is generally not a life-threatening situation…at least not nearly as often as it can be on a motorcycle.

I like to ride a clean motorcycle. This is a matter of preference. I have often heard it said that, "A dirty bike is a ridden bike", so it is clearly not as important to many as it is to me to be on a gleaming, shiny piece of machinery. One reason I bought a Harley-Davidson motorcycle is for its looks. They are beautiful machines and they garner a lot of attention, even more so when the paint is clean and shiny and the chrome gleaming. First, I use a damp "bug scrubber" sponge to clean the windshield, faring, front fender and any forward-facing surfaces. These are the surfaces that are going to have squished insects on them. Then I clean my bike with a spray cleaner/wax that I wipe on with a soft micro-fiber cloth and then buff with a clean micro-fiber cloth. This stuff will leave the windshield and mirrors clean and clear and the paint and chrome sparkling, and you don't have to hose down your bike and dry it. It makes the job easier and faster. There are many good products out there but the best one I found is one that was sold at Honda dealerships. They changed the name a couple of times, but it was originally called "Pro Honda". Lately I have bought the stuff that you will see young men and/or women demonstrating outside convenience stores, and it has worked well.

CHAPTER ELEVEN
TIPS FOR DRIVERS

Since I have spent some considerable time talking about what you should and should not do when operating a motorcycle, I wanted to take a little space here to provide some tips for drivers of vehicles other than motorcycles as well. These tips are not only for non-riders, but for you as well when you are driving your car or truck. The reason for this is that it is *everyone's* responsibility to keep the roadways safe, both for motorcycles and all other vehicles as well.

The first tip is do not follow a motorcycle too closely. Make sure you stay back a full two seconds or more. Remember that a motorcycle needs less distance to stop than a car. If a rider in front of you slams on his brakes quickly he is going to come to a stop before you do. If you are not back enough you are going to plow into him from behind. Also, if a motorcycle takes a spill in front of you there is a better chance of not running him over if you are following at a safe distance.

The second tip is always be aware of motorcycles on the roadway, whether coming toward you or traveling in the same direction as you. Be extra vigilant when changing lanes, making a turn, or entering a roadway. It is at these times that motorcycles are hardest to see. Keep motorcycles out of your blind spots and visible in at least one of your mirrors at all times.

When driving in poor weather conditions, and especially rain, slow down around motorcycles. They are less stable in the rain than you are in your car or truck and they may be traveling slower than the rest of the traffic to compensate and because their visibility is impaired.

Never yield the right of way. This is a good habit regardless of whether or not motorcycles are in the area. You have the right of way for a reason and other drivers expect you to take it and act accordingly. If you yield it you are doing something unexpected by the drivers around you and can likely cause an accident. Often people yield the right of way because they are being polite and allowing someone into or across the traffic flow. This is couteous but if other drivers aren't expecting it and have to compensate for your actions at the last second the results can be tragic. Recently I was in the center lane on a three-lane roadway stopped at a traffic light. There were three or four vehicles in front of me and vehicles lined up on my left hand side as well. When the light turned green all three lanes of traffic started moving forward. All of a sudden a pickup truck on my left decided to stop and let a car coming in the other direction make a left hand turn to cross the street. Because I was on my bike I could not see what was on the other side of the pickup or why he was stopping. The car, carrying two teenage girls, started across the road way and all of a sudden was right in front of me. I slammed on my brakes to avoid hitting them. Now, at this point, the driver of the car did what almost all people do, and is exactly the wrong thing to do. She saw me and hit her brakes, causing her vehicle to stop right in front of me while I am still trying to bring the bike to a stop. Had she hit the gas instead of the brakes she would have gotten her car out of my way enough to get around the back of it. Instead she just created a roadblock, one that I was about to slam into. I yelled at her to keep going and she hit the gas just in time for me to be able to skirt to my left, in front of the "yielder" and avoid hitting her car. Had there been an accident it would not have been my fault or the girl's fault (although she legally would have been at fault as she didn't have the right of way), but the fault of the driver of the pickup who decided to ignore his green light, stop, and let a vehicle cross the road totally unaware of two more lanes of traffic to his right. You have the right of way for a reason, do not yield it.

The next tip relates to the story I told in the last one. Should you find yourself pulling out in front of a moving motorcycle and blocking it, do NOT hit your brakes. Your stopped vehicle just makes the situation worse. Take the quickest escape route available to you and hit the gas. This goes for pulling out in front of a car or truck as well. You especially don't want to be broadsided by one of those.

Riding a motorcycle will make you a better and safer driver of a car or truck. Experiences you gain on the bike will add to your knowledge base of the things other drivers will do and the results that can be caused. Because of that knowledge base you will be better at anticipating what a driver may do than the driver will be at anticipating what a motorcycle may do. Always remember that and always stay vigilant.

CHAPTER TWELVE
SUMMARY

So you have reached the end of this treatise and you have had access to pretty much the sum total of my knowledge regarding learning how to ride a motorcycle, how to buy one, how to stay safe on the road, how to enjoy your riding experience, and how to keep your motorcycle in tip top shape.

However, I want to take a moment and just recap the things I feel are the most important for you to remember, and put into practice.

First, I cannot stress enough the value of taking the Rider's Safety Course and learning how to ride the correct way. I truly believe I could take that course ten times and learn something new each time. You will be so much more prepared for facing the situations that you will encounter on the road with what you learn in this course. Make the investment of a few hundred dollars, it is well worth it, especially if it saves your life.

Wear your safety equipment. It can make a difference in the severity of injury, and might just save your life.

Continue to practice in parking lots and on neighborhood streets before you venture out onto the highways. Sharpen your skills and slowly introduce yourself to traffic situations. Start riding more rural, less traveled roads and work your way to the busier highways.

Be constantly vigilant of other vehicles and what they might do. Practice defensive driving techniques each and every time you are on your motorcycle. Maintain your safety cushion and stay out of drivers' blind spots. Always have a plan for what you will do if an unanticipated event occurs in front of or next to you.

Slow down and practice extra caution in bad weather. Dress for the kind of weather you will be riding in. If the weather is too dangerous stay off your bike.

Keep your bike in the best mechanical shape possible. Treat it with respect and it will pay you dividends you may never be aware of.

The last thing I want to leave you with is that for several years I looked ahead to my retirement and asked myself, "What am I going to do?" I didn't have a real hobby that I enjoyed and I didn't particularly care to travel. When I discovered motorcycle riding at the age of 55 I knew that question was now answered. And, I discovered that I DO care to travel...on the seat of my motorcycle. I have ridden to or through11 states so far, some several times, and I have loved every mile of it. I did not think this would be for me, but I was dead wrong. Don't prejudge whether or not you would enjoy motorcycle riding until you've tried it...you just might *love it!*

CPSIA information can be obtained at www.ICGtesting.com
Printed in the USA
BVOW03s1744300314

349228BV00006B/65/P